D1519927

MISSION TO MARS

THIS EDITION
Editorial Management by Oriel Square
Produced for DK by WonderLab Group LLC
Jennifer Emmett, Erica Green, Kate Hale, *Founders*

Editors Grace Hill Smith, Libby Romero, Maya Myers, Michaela Weglinski;
Photography Editors Kelley Miller, Annette Kiesow, Nicole DiMella; **Managing Editor** Rachel Houghton;
Designers Project Design Company; **Researcher** Michelle Harris; **Copy Editor** Lori Merritt;
Indexer Connie Binder; **Proofreader** Larry Shea; **Reading Specialist** Dr. Jennifer Albro;
Curriculum Specialist Elaine Larson

Published in the United States by DK Publishing
1745 Broadway, 20th Floor, New York, NY 10019

Copyright © 2023 Dorling Kindersley Limited
DK, a Division of Penguin Random House LLC
23 24 25 26 10 9 8 7 6 5 4 3 2 1
001-334079-July/2023

A catalog record for this book
is available from the Library of Congress.
HC ISBN: 978-0-7440-7412-3
PB ISBN: 978-0-7440-7414-7

DK books are available at special discounts when purchased in bulk for sales promotions, premiums,
fundraising, or educational use. For details, contact: DK Publishing Special Markets,
1745 Broadway, 20th Floor, New York, NY 10019
SpecialSales@dk.com

Printed and bound in China

The publisher would like to thank the following for their kind permission to reproduce their images:
a=above; c=center; b=below; l=left; r=right; t=top; b/g=background

Alamy Stock Photo: NASA Image Collection 24tl, 26cla, Stocktrek Images, Inc. / Vernon Lewis Gallery 28tl, Xinhua 39cra;
Depositphotos Inc: Javvani 45cra; **Dreamstime.com:** 3000ad 52tl, Awcnz62 14-15b, Bazuzzza 18tl, Dmitrii Bontsev 19tl,
Matias Del Carmine 15tr, Karina Caverdos Chernenko 10clb, De Agostini / DEA / BIBLIOTECA AMBROSIANA 21tr, Dragoscondrea
60tl, Sergey Drozdov 46tl, Framestock Footages 46-47b, Markus Gann 14tl, Ruslan Gilmanshin 40tl, Haiyin 49cr, Chris Hill 20cr,
Sebastian Kaulitzki 12t, Mike_kiev 60-61, Mikhail Kokhanchikov 16-17t, Jakub Krechowicz 11tr, Artur Maltsau 4-5, Manjik 53tr,
Martin Molcan 48tl, Nerthuz 3cb, Andrew Pavlovich 59tr, Planetfelicity 56br, Mikhail Rudenko 7tr, Konstantin Shaklein 41tr, Andrey
Simonenko 28cl, Nuthawut Somsuk 17cra, Sorapop Udomsri 8tl, Hannu Viitanen 6-7b, 10-11b, Vivilweb 48-49b, Whughes98144 49tr,
Wisconsinart 35b, Rainer Zapka 44; **Getty Images:** AFP / Staff 30-31b, Bettmann 20tl, Sebastien Micke / Paris Match / Contour 57cra,
Jim Watson / AFP 42tl, Moment Unreleased / Max shen 45tr; **Getty Images / iStock:** Marcos Silva 58-59t; **NASA:** 23tr, 50t, 52clb,
AI SpaceFactory / Plomp 52br, ESA / NASA / JPL-Caltech 51tr, ESA / NASA / SOHO 34tl, Regan Geeseman 55tr, Goddard Space Flight
Center 35tr, ICON 56tl, 56cla, JPL 55cr, JPL / NASA 32cla, JPL-Caltech 54, JSC 60clb, Library of Congress 38tl, MAVEN / Lunar and
Planetary Institute 6clb, NASA / GSFC 43br, NASA / JPL 22cla, 23b, 25t, 27t, NASA / JPL / Cornell 30tl, NASA / JPL / Cornell University
31tr, NASA / JPL / KSC / Lockheed Martin Space Systems 13tr, NASA / JPL / MSSS 9cr, 10tl, NASA / JPL / University of Arizona / Los
Alamos National Laboratories 29cr, NASA / JPL-Calech / University of Arizona 32-33b, NASA / JPL-Caltech 37tr, 38-39b, 51bl,
NASA / JPL-Caltech / ASU 38cl, NASA / JPL-Caltech / GSFC / Univ. of Arizona 20clb, NASA / JPL-Caltech / MSSS 9tr, 34br, NASA /
JPL-Caltech / Univ. of Arizona 8b, NASA, NASA / JPL-Caltech / University of Arizona / Texas A&M University 33tr, NASA / JSC 40-41b,
NASA / KSC 24br, 26br, NASA / USGS 13bl, Isaac Watson 58cl; **Science Photo Library:** European Space Agency / D. Ducros 36-37t,
NASA 42-43b, Detlev Van Ravenswaay 28-29b; **Shutterstock.com:** yaruna 18br

Cover images: *Front:* **Shutterstock.com:** Lubo Ivanko (Background), Dima Zel b; *Back:* **Shutterstock.com:** Macrovector bl,
Microstocker.Pro clb, Pike-28 cra, ptashka cl, VWeiner cr

All other images © Dorling Kindersley
For more information see: www.dkimages.com

For the curious
www.dk.com

MISSION TO MARS

Libby Romero

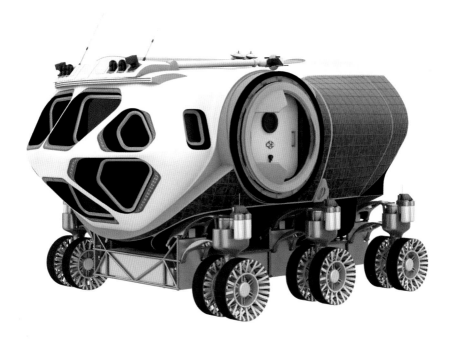

CONTENTS

illustration of an imagined Mars habitat

Measuring Mars

At 4,212 miles (6,779 km) across, Mars is about half as big as Earth and twice as big as our Moon.

Surface Area

Despite the difference in size, Earth and Mars have about the same amount of land surface area. That's because 70 percent of Earth is covered by water.

Major Change

Billions of years ago, Mars looked like Earth. It had rivers, lakes, and maybe even a shallow ocean.

INTRODUCING MARS

Mars is a small, cold, rocky planet. The landscape is a desert covered with giant craters, deep canyons, and extinct volcanoes. Whirlwinds swirl red dust across its surface. Some of these storms look like little tornadoes. Others grow so big they cover the entire planet.

Mars lies between Earth and Jupiter.

Mars

If you were to go to Mars, you couldn't breathe the air. There would be no rivers or lakes to quench your thirst. If you looked up into the sky, you would see two moons. You might be able to see Earth in the distance. You would be standing on Earth's neighbor, the fourth planet from the Sun. And you would be somewhere no human has ever gone before.

Mission to Mars
Plans are underway to send people to Mars. Before that can be done, scientists must develop a spacecraft that can safely carry astronauts on the very long trip to Mars, enter its atmosphere, and fly back to Earth.

Life on Mars
Scientists are searching for signs of life on Mars, now and in the past. They are developing ways humans could survive there in the future.

Earth's Year
Earth is 93 million miles (150 million km) away from the Sun and orbits it in 365.25 days. That is one Earth year.

When people go to Mars, it will be important to think about how Earth and Mars are alike and different. One day on Mars, called a sol, lasts for 24 hours, 37 minutes. Earth's day is 23 hours, 56 minutes —pretty much the same.

Swirling columns of dust and wind called dust devils occur on Mars, too.

A year is quite different, though. One year is how long it takes a planet to orbit the Sun. Mars is more than 142 million miles (228 million km) from the Sun, or about twice as far as Earth is. It takes 687 Earth days to orbit the Sun—about twice as long as it takes Earth.

Seasons on Mars are about twice as long as Earth seasons. But they're different lengths, unlike on Earth, because for most of the year, Mars is far away from the Sun.

Mars is closest to the Sun when it's summer in its Southern Hemisphere. Summer is the shortest and hottest season in that part of the planet. Why? Mars is tilted, just like Earth. During summer, the Southern Hemisphere leans toward the Sun.

If you arrived in spring, you'd see a lot of dust. Dust storms on Mars can be massive, but fortunately, they don't have hurricane-force winds. The fastest winds on Mars travel about 70 miles per hour (113 kph). A gentle breeze is more common.

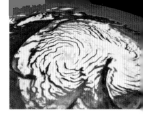

Ice Caps
Mars has polar ice caps. In spring, they recede, or pull back. By summer, they may disappear. They grow back when temperatures drop in the fall.

Snow
Mars has snow! During the Martian winter, snow forms in the atmosphere, a few miles above the surface. But it vaporizes before it reaches the ground.

Global Warming
Huge dust storms, like the one illustrated here, affect temperatures on Mars. There can be a difference in temperature of more than 63 Fahrenheit degrees (35 Celsius degrees) between dusty air and clean air on Mars.

Toxic Air
Another reason you couldn't breathe on Mars is because its atmosphere contains a different mix of gases than Earth's. The air is mostly made of carbon dioxide—a gas we breathe out.

Mars has a very elliptical, or elongated, orbit. Because of that, Mars is close to the Sun for only a short part of its year. That causes extreme differences in temperature. The average temperature on Mars is -80°F (-62°C). But temperatures range from around -200°F (-129°C) at the poles in the winter to 70°F (21°C) closer to the equator in the summer.

One reason people couldn't breathe if they went to Mars is that the Martian atmosphere is about 100 times thinner than Earth's. Earth has a magnetic field that extends from the planet's inner core far out into space. It acts like a shield, turning away solar winds that could otherwise sweep Earth's atmosphere away.

Earth's gravity holds the atmosphere in place. Mars has only small patches of magnetic crust. And it has about a third as much gravity as Earth. It's pretty easy for solar winds to make Mars's atmosphere disappear.

illustration of Mars landscape

Gravity
If you weighed 100 pounds (45 kg) on Earth, you would only weigh 38 pounds (17 kg) on Mars.

Ozone
Mars has three separate ozone layers. But they are so thin that they do little to block the Sun's ultraviolet light.

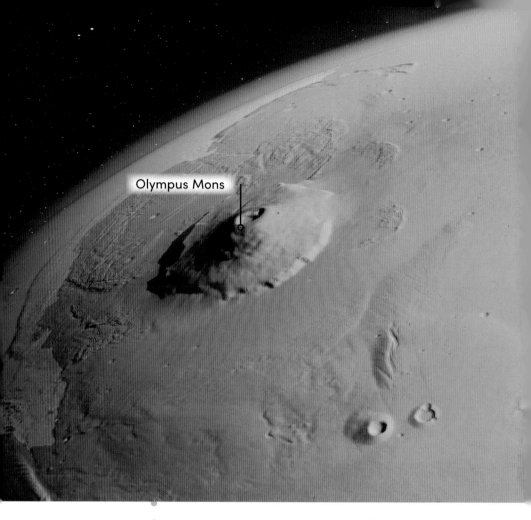
Olympus Mons

Raising a Giant
Olympus Mons wouldn't have been able to grow so big on Earth. Volcanoes erupt more often on Mars, and Mars has less gravity to pull down on growing volcanoes than Earth does.

If you had time to explore Mars, you'd see some pretty spectacular features on the Martian surface. Olympus Mons is the biggest volcano in our solar system. It rises 16 miles (26 km) high, and its base is nearly as wide as the state of Arizona in the US.

Valles Marineris is the largest canyon. It's over 2,500 miles (4,000 km) long, 372 miles (600 km) wide, and 4 miles (6 km) deep. That makes Earth's Grand Canyon look like a shallow ditch!

How do we know so much about Mars? We've studied it for years. We've sent robotic explorers there, too. The next step is for people to go to Mars. Before we do, though, we need to learn as much about Mars as we can. That's the only way we will be able to reach Mars safely and survive after we get there.

Valles Marineris

Perfect Timing
The best time to travel to Mars, called the launch window, is when Earth and Mars are as close to each other as possible. But the one-way trip will still take between four and seven months!

ANCIENT BELIEFS

Mars is one of the planets you can see from Earth without a telescope. Long ago, when people looked up into the night sky, they saw a dark canvas covered with twinkling lights—and one fiery red ball that took its own strange path across the horizon. That ball was Mars.

In 400 BCE, ancient Babylonians were some of the first people to study that red ball in the sky.

The Red Planet
The soil on Mars looks red because iron minerals in it rust. Because of that, people call Mars the Red Planet.

They believed that their gods sent messages about the future through celestial bodies. This ball was red, a color they associated with anger and evil, so they named it Nergal, after their god of war, death, and destruction.

The Babylonians studied all sorts of astronomical events. They kept track of their observations and used them to create a calendar. It had a week with seven days—just like the calendar we use today. Their Tuesday was "Mars Day."

Mars Day
In French, the word for Tuesday is *mardi*. In Italian, it is *martedi*. And in Spanish, it is *martes*. And in Old English, Tiu was the Germanic god of the sky and war. In many languages, Tuesday is still named after the god of war.

ancient Babylonia

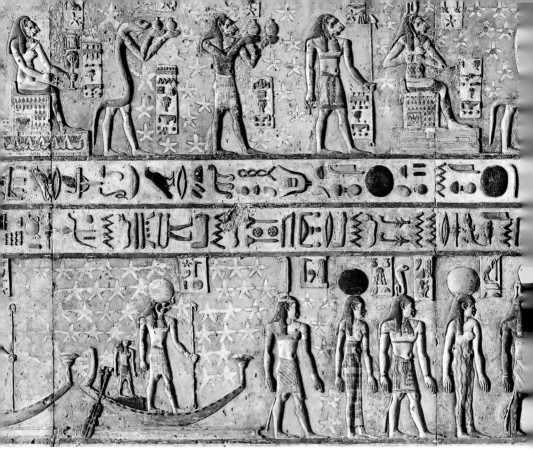

Honoring Mars

In ancient Egyptian art, the god representing Mars was often a winged falcon with three snake heads.

Ancient Egyptians studied the sky, too. One thing they noticed was five bright objects—which we now know are planets—that behaved differently from everything else. They named these objects after versions of Horus, their falcon god of the sky. Mars was "Har Decher," or "The Red One," in honor of its rosy hue.

March

1	2	3	4	5	6	7
8	9	10	11	12	13	14
15	16	17	18	19	20	21
22	23	24	25	26	27	28
29	30	31				

The Month of Mars
The month of March is named after the god Mars. In ancient Rome, March was the time when farmers returned to their fields and soldiers returned to the battlefield.

To ancient Greeks and Romans, the red ball in the sky represented war. In fact, both named the planet after their gods of war. For the Greeks, that was Ares—a god they depicted as either beautiful and courageous or a hateful, murderous coward. For the Romans, it was Mars—an honorable and mighty warrior who protected Rome and the Roman way of life.

EARLY DISCOVERIES

Mars has played an important role in our understanding of the universe. In the second century CE, Greek mathematician and astronomer Claudius Ptolemy created a model of the universe. He placed Earth in the middle, with everything else revolving around it. For more than a thousand years, people believed this was how the universe worked.

Ptolemy's model of the universe

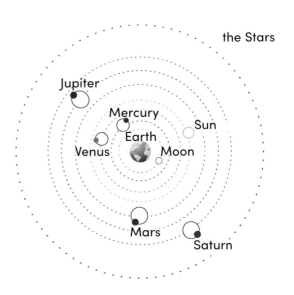

Copernicus's model of the universe

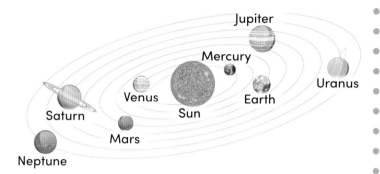

In 1543, Polish mathematician and astronomer Nicolaus Copernicus published a book that contained a new idea. He said that Earth and the other planets revolved around the Sun.

At this time, followers of the Catholic Church still believed that everything revolved around Earth. That made Copernicus's idea very controversial, and the Church banned his book. But Copernicus's ideas sparked a flame, and scientists later proved that his theory was true.

Orbital Answer

Johannes Kepler, Brahe's assistant, solved the puzzle of Mars's orbit. Planets have elliptical, not round, orbits. And they orbit the Sun, not Earth. Because Earth completes its orbit faster, it passes Mars on its trip around the Sun. This makes it look like Mars is going backward.

The First Telescope

Galileo Galilei often gets credit for inventing the telescope. But a Dutch eyeglass maker named Hans Lippershey was the first to apply for a patent. Galileo's later telescope was strong enough for people to view objects in space.

Martian Moons

Asaph Hall named Mars's moons Phobos and Deimos, after the sons of the Greek war god, Ares.

GALILEO GALILEI

In 1609, Italian astronomer Galileo Galilei did something nobody had ever done before. He used a telescope to see objects in space. Although Galileo observed Mars through his telescope, his studies focused on other areas. It was up to other astronomers to learn about Mars.

In 1659, Dutch astronomer Christiaan Huygens noted a large, dark spot on Mars. By tracking the spot's movement, he calculated that Mars has a 24-hour day. Other scientists later calculated the Mars day even more precisely.

As telescopes improved, astronomers continued to learn more about Mars. They saw white spots at the planet's South Pole and yellow clouds above its surface. They created maps of Martian continents and seas. Astronomer Asaph Hall discovered that Mars has two moons.

Martian Misconception
In 1877, Italian astronomer Giovanni Schiaparelli made a map of the Martian surface. It included straight channels, which he called "canali." Schiaparelli knew they were natural features, but other people didn't. They thought he meant there were canals on Mars, and something was up there to build them.

THE FIRST MISSIONS TO MARS

It wasn't until the twentieth century that massive advances in technology allowed scientists to take the next giant leap—sending a spacecraft to Mars. On July 14, 1965, the National Aeronautics and Space Administration's (NASA) Mariner 4 flew just 6,000 miles (9,800 km) from Mars.

The Mariner Program
NASA's Mariner program consisted of 10 small robotic spacecraft, three of which—Mariners 4, 6, and 7—flew by Mars. Mariner 9 orbited the Red Planet.

Mariner 4 sent the first close-up pictures of Mars back to Earth. The photos showed deep craters, like those on Earth's Moon. The spacecraft's instruments took measurements showing that Mars is very cold, has a thin atmosphere, and has no magnetic field surrounding it.

Mariner 6 and Mariner 7 reached Mars in 1969. They flew closer to Mars than Mariner 4 had, used better cameras, and took more pictures. But because of where they traveled, their photos showed only craters on the surface, too.

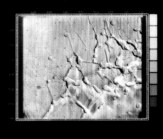

In 1971, NASA launched Mariner 9. Unlike previous Mariners, which were designed to fly by Mars, it orbited Mars for almost a year.

When Mariner 9 arrived, Mars was covered with a great dust storm. After the dust settled, the spacecraft took pictures of the entire Martian surface. They revealed gigantic volcanoes, massive canyons, and ancient riverbeds. They also gave us the first close-up photos of Mars's two moons.

Mariner 6

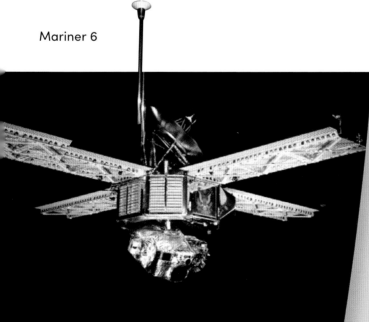

Through the Lens
Mariner photos proved that there were no canals on Mars. They also gave us our first views of Olympus Mons and Valles Marineris, which is seen here.

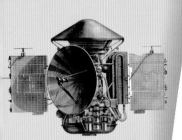

Observing Mars from a distance was interesting, but scientists wanted more. They wanted to get to the surface, and in 1976, Viking 1 and Viking 2 did just that.

The two identical spacecraft each had an orbiter and a lander. After entering the Mars orbit, the spacecraft separated. Their orbiters stayed in space, while their landers touched down on the surface.

assembling a Viking orbiter and lander

first photo taken from the Mars lander Viking 1

The Viking missions had several objectives: photograph the surface of Mars, learn more about its atmosphere and surface, and search for evidence of life. Although neither lander found traces of life, their experiments did reveal that Mars has volcanic soil and a thin, dry carbon dioxide atmosphere. They also discovered water on Mars in solid and vapor forms. This opened up the possibility that life might have existed on Mars long ago.

Expiration Date
The Viking mission was designed to last for 90 days. It lasted for six years.

Probable Cause
Investigators think the Mars Observer failed after a fuel line ruptured, sending it into a spin.

THE NEXT ERA OF EXPLORATION

It would be almost 20 years before NASA approached Mars again. In 1992, it launched the Mars Observer orbiter. Unfortunately, ground control lost contact with the spacecraft three days before it was supposed to enter orbit around Mars.

This rocket carried Mars Global Surveyor into space. It was the first successful mission to Mars in two decades.

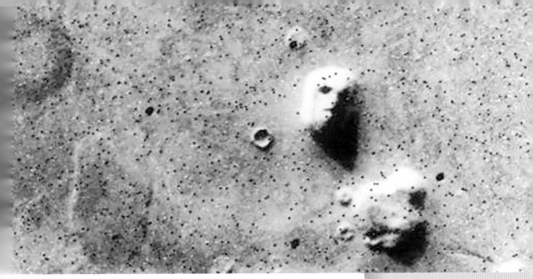

The next orbiter, Mars Global Surveyor, had much better results. It entered Mars's orbit in early September 1997, and it studied the planet for nearly a decade. By the time it stopped working in 2006, it had returned more information than all the previous Martian missions combined.

The spacecraft took pictures of ancient deltas and recent gullies—signs of water on the Red Planet. The data it collected helped scientists understand weather patterns on Mars and create 3D maps of its surface. It also detected mineral deposits that helped scientists find safe landing sites for future missions to Mars.

The Face
A Viking 1 orbiter photo of Mars showed a feature that looked like a human face. Some people imagined that it was an alien artifact. Mars Global Surveyor photos proved the site was only a big, flat-topped hill.

Sojourner Name
The Sojourner rover was named after civil rights activist Sojourner Truth.

Sojourner's Journey
The Sojourner rover traveled about 330 feet (100 m) altogether, but it never ventured more than 39 feet (12 m) from Pathfinder.

On July 4, 1997, parachutes opened, airbags deployed, and a pyramid-shaped lander named Pathfinder floated toward the surface of Mars. Soon after, a robotic rover about the size of a microwave emerged from the spacecraft. The rover was Sojourner, the first wheeled robot on Mars.

Pathfinder sat still, collecting information about wind and weather. It sent 16,500 photos back to Earth. Sojourner explored. It sent back more than 550 additional pictures, along with evidence that Mars used to be much warmer and wetter than it is today.

NASA launched the Mars Odyssey orbiter in 2001. About five months after its arrival, instruments aboard Odyssey detected large amounts of hydrogen in the Martian soil. To scientists, that was a sign that there could be ice beneath the surface. Seven years later, Odyssey identified salt deposits on Mars. These only appear in places where there was once a lot of water.

illustration of Pathfinder and Sojourner on Mars

Failed Attempts
NASA attempted two other missions to Mars between the Pathfinder/Sojourner and Odyssey missions. One crashed upon landing. A communication error caused the other to fall into the Martian atmosphere and break apart.

Going Strong
As of 2022, the Odyssey orbiter is still circling Mars, as shown in this illustration. It is the longest continually active spacecraft to orbit any planet other than Earth.

In Living Color
Spirit and Opportunity were the first rovers to send color pictures of Mars back to Earth.

The European Space Agency and the Italian Space Agency launched Mars Express in 2003. This orbiter is still circling Mars, too. It has discovered even more evidence of water on Mars—minerals that could only form if liquid water had been present.

Mars Express has also found layers of water ice beneath the surface, huge permafrost plains around the South Pole, and methane in the Martian atmosphere.

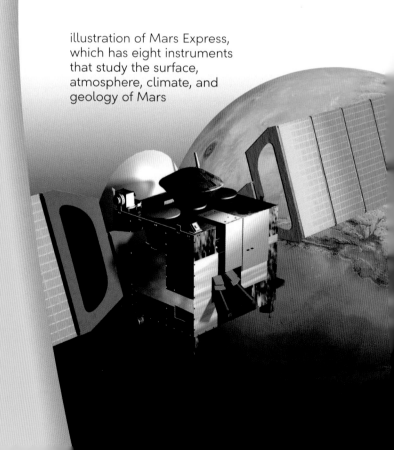

illustration of Mars Express, which has eight instruments that study the surface, atmosphere, climate, and geology of Mars

When you find methane on Earth, it means that active volcanoes or biochemical processes, like photosynthesis, are occurring. On Mars, this could be a sign that tiny microbes are living in the rocks beneath the surface!

In January 2004, twin rovers Spirit and Opportunity arrived on Mars. Their mission was to search for clues about the history of water on Mars.

The rovers landed on opposite sides of the planet. Spirit explored a site that might have been an ancient lake. Opportunity studied what once could have been the shoreline of a salty sea. Both rovers found minerals that only exist where water flows on Earth. Both also found evidence that conditions could have been right to support tiny living organisms long ago.

Getting Bigger
Spirit and Opportunity were each about the size of a golf cart— much larger than Sojourner, the first rover on Mars.

Rover Names
NASA held an essay contest to find names for its twin rovers. Nine-year-old Sofi Collis wrote the winning essay.

Lost and Found
On January 16, 2015, the MRO (illustrated below) found the Beagle 2 lander, which had arrived in 2003 with Mars Express. The lander failed to function after it reached the surface.

New Information
Recently, the MRO discovered that most of the water on Mars disappeared two billion years ago—a billion years later than scientists thought.

By now, scientists knew that there was once plenty of water on Mars. But did that water support life? When and how did the water disappear? Is there water on Mars today? In 2006, the Mars Reconnaissance Orbiter (MRO) began circling the planet to find the answers.

The MRO hasn't found traces of ancient life, but it has located places where tiny microbes could have survived. It has tracked the Martian water cycle. It has also found strong evidence that very salty water flows on Mars today.

In 2008, Phoenix touched down on the frozen northern plains of Mars. It was the first stationary lander to successfully touch down on the planet since the Viking missions more than 30 years before.

Phoenix took panoramic photos of its landing site. It collected icy soil with its long robotic arm and analyzed the samples with tiny ovens and a portable lab. The lander worked for five months. Then, winter set in. Days got shorter, and there wasn't enough sunlight for Phoenix to power its solar panels. It shut down.

illustration of the Phoenix lander on Mars

Melting on Mars
In 2008, the Phoenix lander dug a small trench in the Martian surface. Photos showed hard, bright material in the soil. Four days later, the spots were gone. Scientists confirmed that the spots were water ice, which had evaporated.

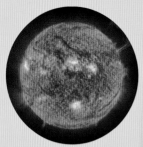

Solar Power
Radiation is a form of energy from the Sun, and high levels are dangerous to people. Astronauts would experience high levels of radiation on the trip to Mars, but on the surface of Mars, radiation levels are about the same as they are on the International Space Station.

Next up was the Curiosity rover, which landed in a giant Martian crater in 2012. Curiosity is as big as a small SUV. It has 17 cameras, a laser, a drill, and a robotic arm that can hold a camera and send a selfie back to Earth.

Curiosity's self-portrait

Among Curiosity's amazing discoveries is a type of carbon, found in the soil samples it collected. On Earth, carbon is a sign of life. Scientists aren't sure whether it means the same thing on Mars. Curiosity is still on the move, and until its plutonium power source runs out, it will continue to explore Mars.

In 2014, NASA's MAVEN orbiter began the first mission dedicated to studying the planet's upper atmosphere. Through MAVEN, scientists discovered that warm temperatures and strong winds cause water vapor to rise extremely high into Mars's atmosphere. There, ultraviolet rays from the Sun break water into its parts—hydrogen and oxygen molecules—which float into space. This explains what happened to the deep ocean that covered Mars billions of years ago. It was lost to space.

MAVEN Name
MAVEN is an acronym. It stands for Mars Atmosphere and Volatile Evolution.

Measuring MAVEN
MAVEN is about as long as a school bus and weighs about as much as a full-size SUV.

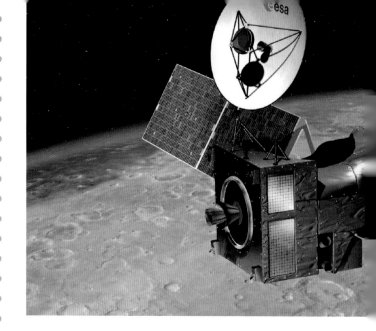

Dust Buster
In 2019, MAVEN, the Trace Gas Orbiter, and the MRO all studied a small dust storm on Mars. It was the first time so many spacecraft had studied the same event.

In 2016, the European Space Agency's ExoMars Trace Gas Orbiter joined MAVEN in orbit around Mars. ExoMars is searching for gases in the atmosphere, like methane, that would be potential signs of life on Mars.

Living organisms on Earth release methane when they digest food. Earlier missions to Mars detected methane on its surface. So far, the Trace Gas Orbiter hasn't found any in the atmosphere.

After decades of studying the surface and atmosphere of Mars, the InSight lander, which set down in 2018, is giving scientists a more detailed look inside the Red Planet.

illustration of ExoMars
Trace Gas Orbiter

Its instruments record ground vibrations, read the soil temperature, and measure how much Mars wobbles as it orbits the Sun.

InSight is using seismic waves to reveal new details about the three layers of Mars: a massive, liquid inner core; a thin mantle; and a layered, solid crust. Mars's crust doesn't have tectonic plates like Earth's does, so no new crust has been created since the planet was formed about 4.5 billion years ago.

A Helping Hand
Ingenuity quickly tackled its original mission—proving that rotorcraft could fly in Mars's thin atmosphere. It now acts as a scout, flying ahead to find the best path for the Perseverance rover to follow.

In 2021, the Perseverance rover landed on Mars. It carried a passenger, a tiny helicopter called Ingenuity. Ingenuity made the first powered flight on any world beyond Earth.

To help people survive on Mars one day, Perseverance is testing a method of getting oxygen from the Martian atmosphere. It's also finding resources people could use. Working with Ingenuity, Perseverance is locating natural hazards that would put future astronauts in danger.

Perseverance has also been drilling into the soil, collecting samples, and storing the samples in tubes. Future spacecraft will bring the tubes back to Earth for testing. Scientists hope that the evidence will prove that life once existed on Mars.

Mars is one of the most studied planets in our solar system. As of 2022, three rovers and one lander are exploring Mars on the surface, and eight spacecraft are studying it from above. It is an international effort, with a number of countries working together to learn more about the Red Planet.

Monumental Touchdown
With the success of its Zhurong rover, China became the second country to successfully land a spacecraft on the surface of Mars.

illustration of Perseverance (left) and Ingenuity (right)

Artemis Name
The Artemis program is named after the Greek goddess of the Moon. NASA's program that first took astronauts to the Moon was named after her twin brother, Apollo.

MOON TO MARS

People are explorers. We have traveled across the continents, under the sea, and to the Moon. It's in our nature to want to see more. So, it makes sense that after sending spacecraft to fly by, go around, and set down on Mars, humans would want to go there themselves. The program designed to accomplish that is called Artemis.

Artemis is a collaboration between the US and a growing list of other countries and private companies.

illustration of NASA's Orion crew capsule headed to the Moon

The first step was Artemis 1, which launched on November 16, 2022. This uncrewed flight flew thousands of miles past the Moon before returning to Earth. A second mission—Artemis 2— will conduct a similar flight in 2024. Then, astronauts will be on board. A year later, Artemis 3 would take astronauts back to the Moon. Four astronauts would ride in the Orion spacecraft, which would launch on NASA's new rocket, the Space Launch System (SLS). Two astronauts would then transfer to a SpaceX Starship landing vehicle, which would take them to the Moon.

Major Boost
The Space Launch System is one of the most powerful rockets ever built.

The Crew
One goal of the Artemis 3 mission is to land the first woman and first person of color on the Moon.

In the Works
Three private companies—Blue Origin, Dynetics, and SpaceX—are developing Human Landing Systems for the Artemis program.

Lunar Base
The Artemis Base Camp will have office and living space. There will also be lunar terrain vehicles that astronauts can drive on the Moon.

Future Artemis missions would carry astronauts into space. One of their first jobs would be to construct an outpost called Gateway, which would orbit the Moon.

At the outpost, astronauts plan to dock the Human Landing System that would take them back and forth to the Moon. They would refill supplies during longer missions, and they would conduct scientific investigations that could help them with later missions to Mars. In time, the Gateway outpost would serve as a staging point for deep-space flight to the Red Planet.

Astronauts don't plan to return to the Moon until Artemis 3 blasts off. On this and other early missions, they would live and work in their lander's pressurized crew cabin for up to a week.

Eventually, astronauts would build the Artemis Base Camp at the Moon's South Pole. The fixed habitat would have everything that up to four astronauts would need for a monthlong stay. Astronauts plan to test new tools and equipment that could be used on Mars. Scientists would study how their bodies respond to living in deep space.

The Right Stuff
The Moon's South Pole is the ideal place to build a base camp. It has ice and other minerals astronauts could use.

Someday, astronauts might live and work on the Moon, as shown in this illustration.

South Pole

illustration of a rocket on Mars

If everything goes according to plan, sustainable operations would be possible on the Moon by the end of the 2020s. That opens the door for the journey to Mars. Both the US and China hope to send humans to the Red Planet by the mid-2030s.

But there's a huge difference between traveling to the Moon and traveling to Mars. One is distance. It takes astronauts a few days to get to the Moon and land on its surface. It takes many months to reach Mars. That's a long time for humans to risk exposure to radiation in space.

Several spacecraft have flown to Mars. But none of them have carried people and all of the supplies they would need to survive there. All of these things add weight, as does the huge amount of fuel required to transport them such a distance—and get them home to Earth. To take off, the spacecraft would need to be light enough to overcome Earth's gravity. Right now, we don't have the technology needed to safely make the trip.

Base Model
This model, built in a wilderness area in Jinchuan, China, shows what China's base camp on Mars might look like.

Time to Sleep
According to a study by the European Space Agency, putting astronauts into hibernation could be the best way for them to stay healthy while traveling to Mars. Sleeping astronauts would need less food and space, so spacecraft size and weight would be reduced, too.

A Soft Landing
Just before the Perseverance rover landed on Mars in 2021, a special camera examined the surface. It found the safest spot to land. Future missions will use this same technology when they go to the Red Planet, as imagined in the illustration above.

Getting to Mars won't be easy, and many challenges remain. But breakthroughs happen all the time. For instance, it takes a lot of power for a spacecraft to fly such a great distance. NASA is investigating nuclear-based options that could work.

And recently, engineers in Canada say they have developed a laser-based system that heats hydrogen fuel—and could send a crew to Mars in just 45 days! Fast is good, but safety is the priority.

That's why setting up a base on the Moon first is such an important step. On the Moon, astronauts can test new systems and technologies. They can see how living in space for longer periods of time affects their bodies. They can learn how to survive in an environment so vastly different from Earth's.

Taking the Heat
Heat shields protect spacecraft as they enter an atmosphere. Typically, they are made of rigid metals. NASA engineers developed a stronger, lighter type of heat shield that will unfold when needed.

This illustration shows what it might be like for astronauts to walk on Mars.

Perfect Conditions

Earth is known as a Goldilocks planet. It's not too hot and not too cold. That makes it possible for water to exist in all three states—solid, liquid, and gas.

Imperfect Conditions

Conditions on Mars—a weaker gravitational pull, trace amounts of oxygen, and higher radiation levels—could change the human body. When astronaut Scott Kelly lived on the International Space Station for a year, he grew 2 inches (5 cm).

LIVING AND WORKING ON MARS

Earth has everything humans need to survive: food, water, oxygen—even protection from the Sun. Mars has none of that. It's very far away, too. That would make it hard for people to get the supplies they need to build things. So, how exactly are people supposed to live and work on Mars?

This illustration shows what a future colony on Mars might look like.

First, let's take a look at food. To survive on Mars long term, humans on Mars would need to grow their own food.

On Earth, we can plant seeds. Not so on Mars. The atmosphere, soil, and even gravity are different. Space farmers would likely grow food underground in tanks filled with a special solution. Or they could use greenhouses. Scientists are investigating ways to grow food from microbes. They've also found a way to add oxygen to plants so they could grow in the Martian soil.

Overcoming Low Gravity
In lower gravity, water behaves differently. It doesn't flow from the roots to the leaves of plants like it does on Earth.

3D-Printed Food
People could also use a 3D printer to make food on Mars. Oil and water would be mixed with nutrients stored as powders, liquids, or pastes.

This illustration shows how a robotic system could get water out of Martian soil.

A Better Flush
NASA developed a new toilet for deep-space missions. It will recover 98 percent of the water it uses.

Another problem to tackle would be how to make water. It's expensive to fly water from Earth to the International Space Station, so astronauts there recover water from any source they can—showers, toilets, sinks, and even their own pee. A device called the Water Recovery System recycles the water, making it clean to use again and keeping resupplies to a minimum.

Another approach would be to use resources found on Mars. People could melt ice to make water. Or they could heat hydrated minerals—minerals that have water chemically bound to them—to pull out the water.

Another essential item is oxygen. People won't be able to breathe the air on Mars. There's not enough oxygen, and there's way too much carbon dioxide for us to survive. Enter the Mars Oxygen In-Situ Resource Utilization Experiment, or MOXIE for short.

This little device is one of the instruments on the Perseverance rover. Essentially, it breathes like a tree, inhaling carbon dioxide and exhaling the oxygen we need. And it works! With it, people would be able to make oxygen on Mars.

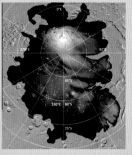

Dusty Mirage
In 2018, scientists thought they had found a huge meltwater lake about a mile beneath Mars's South Pole. But a new study says it was merely a reflection from the volcanic surface.

Bigger Is Better
The MOXIE device currently on Mars is a test model, about the size of a car battery. Once people arrive on Mars, they will need a system that is about 200 times bigger.

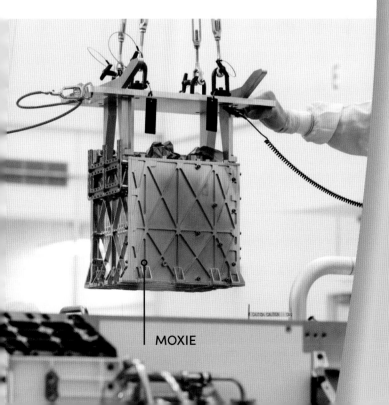

MOXIE

Different Demands
On Earth, buildings are designed to withstand wind and gravity. On Mars, challenges for buildings like the one in this illustration include internal air pressure and extreme changes in temperature.

People on Mars would need safe places to live and work. This is another area where 3D printing could come in handy. Space agencies and companies would send all the required machinery to Mars. If people arrive, they'll use raw materials collected on Mars to build habitats.

A MARSHA prototype has been built on Earth. This illustration shows what it might look like if astronauts built the habitat on Mars.

Extreme Protection
The xEMU will keep astronauts comfortable in temperatures from 250 °F to −250 °F (121 °C to −157 °C).

NASA held a contest challenging companies to come up with the best design for a Mars habitat. The winner was a tall, egg-shaped building called MARSHA. It has wet and dry labs, space for exercise and a garden, and safety features like radiation shields to protect people from the Sun's harmful rays.

Of course, people wouldn't want to stay inside all the time. They'd need spacesuits to protect them when they went outside.

For future missions to the Moon, NASA has developed a new spacesuit called the Exploration Extravehicular Mobility Unit suit, or xEMU. The spacesuit is safer and more flexible than older models. It's also filled with high-tech features, including voice-activated microphones and a remote control system built into the gloves. This same spacesuit might be used for missions to Mars.

Terraforming
Scientists are looking into terraforming, or changing the environment on Mars to make it habitable for humans. There is no guarantee this will work.

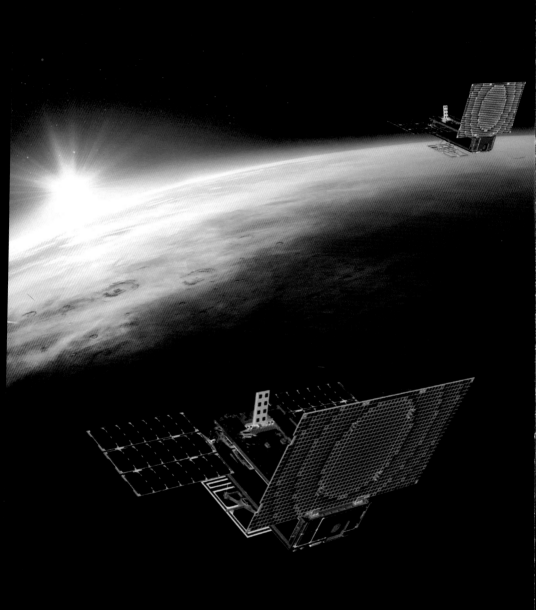

To move around on the Martian surface or carry cargo, astronauts would drive the Space Exploration Vehicle (SEV). The SEV has a pressurized cabin, which means astronauts wouldn't need to wear spacesuits as they traveled. The cabin tilts, giving passengers access to hard-to-see places. The SEV's wheels pivot 360 degrees, allowing it to drive in any direction. It can also walk sideways, like a crab, making it easier to maneuver over bumpy ground.

Communication would be another challenge. Rovers and landers on Mars now beam radio signals back to Earth. It takes between four and 24 minutes for a message to make the trip, depending on the position of the planets.

Delays like this cause problems. If people get to Mars, NASA plans to use lasers to beam messages to and from Earth. This would get the word out 10 to 100 times faster.

This illustration shows MarCO CubeSats, small satellites that communicate with each other. They could also help messages from Mars get to Earth faster.

Cabin Space
The SEV is designed for a crew of two, but four people can fit inside in an emergency.

Zipping Along
NASA says it might take nine weeks to send a map of Mars to Earth with radio signals. With lasers, as imagined in this illustration, it could arrive in nine days.

Practice Run
To study how people will cope with the challenges of living on Mars, NASA used a 3D printer to create a Martian habitat, like the one illustrated here, inside the Johnson Space Center in Houston, Texas, USA. Volunteers will be paid to live there for a year.

BECOME A MARTIAN EXPLORER

Imagine what it would be like to be a Martian explorer. Now, open your eyes and face reality. Traveling to Mars—especially on one of the first missions—would be extremely isolating. You would be millions of miles away from your family and friends, stuck in a small space with five or six other people. It would be the same five or six people every day for years.

In addition to top-notch people skills, you would need technical skills—most likely in more than one area. If something broke, one of you would have to know how to fix it. Not everyone is cut out to be a Martian explorer. But for those who are, a trip to the Red Planet could be a grand adventure.

Becoming an astronaut is no easy task. All NASA astronauts have a master's degree or higher in a STEM (science, technology, engineering, and math) field. Some have spent at least 1,000 hours behind the controls as the pilot-in-command of a jet aircraft. Many served as pilots in the military. And their bodies are in tip-top shape. They have to pass NASA's vigorous long-duration astronaut physical.

Want to Be an Astronaut? Each year, thousands of people apply to be an astronaut. Only a handful get picked.

This illustration shows what it might be like for an astronaut to explore the surface of Mars.

illustration of future Mars colony

Space Tech
There are plenty
of space-related
jobs now—but
they're mostly
on Earth.

Fortunately, there could be lots of other kinds of opportunities to live and work on Mars in the future. NASA, SpaceX, and Blue Origin have already put out word for the types of people they're looking for. It's quite an assortment of talents.

The first task on Mars would be setting up infrastructure—all the buildings and systems people need to survive. Jobs in construction, mining, and manufacturing would be filled first.

A support system of people to cook, clean, and help maintain facilities would be required, too.

Once the community got up and running, the doors would be open for all sorts of fields. Explorers would travel around Mars, making new discoveries. Surveyors would map the land. Technicians and engineers would set up new outposts and make repairs.

All Aboard! SpaceX was the first private company to launch astronauts to the International Space Station. It is building a giant new rocket system that could carry people to Mars.

Protein Sources
Researchers say it's impractical to ship animals to Mars. But many people want to eat meat. Where will they get it? Insects and lab-grown meat!

Going to Mars
"Mars is there, waiting to be reached."
—Edwin "Buzz" Aldrin, Apollo 11 astronaut and second person to walk on the Moon

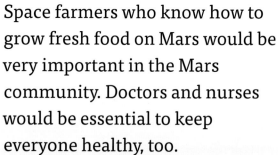

Space farmers who know how to grow fresh food on Mars would be very important in the Mars community. Doctors and nurses would be essential to keep everyone healthy, too.

If more people went to Mars, teachers would fill an important role. They would make sure everyone had the skills needed to live and survive on Mars. They would also educate people about their new surroundings.

In time, there could be a place on Mars for many of the jobs currently done on Earth.

If you envision a mission to Mars in your future, dream big! Learn about Mars and follow your passion. There could be a place for you on the Red Planet.

illustration of future garden on Mars

GLOSSARY

Astronaut
A person trained to live and work in space

Astronomer
A scientist who studies the planets, stars, and space

Atmosphere
A thick layer of gases that surrounds Earth

Delta
A triangular-shaped piece of land at the mouth of a river

Gravity
A force of attraction that pulls objects toward Earth

Lander
A spacecraft designed to land on a body in space

Magnetic field
The space around a planet where the magnetic force is active

Molecule
The smallest unit of a substance that has all the characteristics of that substance

Moon
A natural object that travels around a bigger natural object in space

Orbit
To move continuously around something in space

Orbiter
A spacecraft that orbits a body in space without landing on its surface

Outpost
A settlement in a faraway place

Planet
A large, round object that revolves around a star

Radiation
Energy sent out by heat, light, or a radioactive material

Revolve
To circle around something or move in an orbit

Rocket
A vehicle used to launch people and objects into space

Rotate
To spin or turn in a circle

Rover
A vehicle that explores the surface of a planet or moon

Sol
A Martian day

Solar wind
The constant stream of particles from the Sun

Tectonic plates
Massive pieces of Earth's crust and upper mantle layer that move very slowly

Theory
A group of ideas that explains how or why something happens

Ultraviolet
Light beyond the violet end of the visible light spectrum

INDEX

QUIZ

Answer the questions to see what you have learned. Check your answers in the key below.

1. Why is a year on Mars much longer than a year on Earth?

2. What is Olympus Mons?

3. Who figured out why Mars appears to travel backward every two years?

4. What was the first spacecraft to send pictures of Mars back to Earth?

5. Which missions sent the first spacecraft to the surface of Mars?

6. True or False: There has never been water on the surface of Mars.

7. Where will astronauts in the Artemis program go before going to Mars?

8. What is an xEMU?

1. Mars has a longer orbit around the Sun 2. The largest volcano on Mars and in the solar system 3. Johannes Kepler 4. Mariner 4 5. Viking 1 and Viking 2 6. False 7. The Moon 8. A spacesuit